How To Be a Good Husband and Father

Qualities of a Nice Companion That Tell He's Marriage Material

Mary N. Wilson

TABLE OF CONTENT

INTRODUCTION

Each man needs to be a decent dad and a superior spouse, yet how would you be a decent dad and husband to your significant other and kids is some of the time a secret! Sure a decent father joke helps, however what else could there be to be a decent father? We are sharing noteworthy stages and privileged insights to be a decent dad and spouse today!

The most effective method to be a decent dad and spouse, what each wife wish to be aware of:

I think while raising a family spouses and fathers frequently get so up to speed in the reality of reasoning that they need to give their very best for attempt and deal with their family monetarily and accommodate them. Yet, some of the time with regards to being a decent spouse and father it is considerably more straightforward than that. We are sharing the things that make a decent father and spouse according to the viewpoint of their significant other.

Each spouse can concur that setting priorities makes for a decent dad. Each spouse maintains that the family should be at the highest point of their significant other's need list. This causes them to feel like they are adored and required.

CHAPTER ONE

How To Be a Decent Spouse and Father

1.Play Video

Indeed, we realize that things come up and a few things will overshadow us on occasion, we are not saying that. However, we are saying that we couldn't want anything more than to realize that we are vital exaggerating computer games until very late into the evening.

Significant stage: Record your needs and assess them. In the event that they are not what you are trusting they are, make changes to get them to where you believe that they should be.

2.Be positive

Fathers, kindly be positive. To most mothers, it is the most depleting thing on the planet to have cynicism surrounding them. Toward the finish of a drawn out day, the last thing they need to hear is the reason the clothing is still on the table or that the light was left on higher up once more.
This goes for the children as well. Children will commit errors. Revision of youngsters needs to occur, yet consistently build up the positive by the day's end.

Significant stage: Be more certain for one day. Perceive how that influences everybody around you. For each pessimistic point you make or think you need to express 3 positive things about that individual or circumstance.

3.Offer Thanks for your significant other and kids

Life is a gift. If you somehow happened to die at the present time or your better half or children do, what might they bear in mind by the things you say and do? Could they know how you value them and what they mean to you in your life?

Significant stage: Show in significant ways how much your family means to you. Tell them and show them. Offer thanks for even the seemingly insignificant details that you love about them.

4.Incorporate your Significant other

Your significant other needs to be remembered for independent direction. Allow her assistance to design the financial plan as well as other family choices. She needs to feel required and heard with regards to things in this division.

Significant stage: On the off chance that you are not previously including your better half, ask her what she needs to be remembered for and plunk down and discuss family choices together.

5.Truly Stand by listening to What Your Significant other and Children Say

The main method for being a decent dad and spouse is to listen truly. At the point when your children converse with you, look at them without flinching and pay attention to what they are talking about. Set aside all interruptions and spotlight on what they are talking about.

In the event that they are sharing an issue or battle, don't attempt to settle it, stand by listening to them work all through it as they talk with you. Here and there they simply should be heard.
Exactly the same thing goes for your significant other. Here and there she simply needs to be heard.

Noteworthy stage: The following time your significant other and kids converse with you truly pay attention to what they are talking about and what they need from you. 9/10 they will let you know if you tune in for it.

6. Show Love Transparently

Show your better half and children love transparently. Kiss your significant other, hold her hand, sit by her on the love seat. Show love for her transparently so she knows no ifs, ands or buts the amount you love her. The equivalent goes for your children. Let them know you love them. Give your children clench hand knocks or set up secret handshakes in the event that they don't need embraces from you.

Significant stage: show every individual from your family love straightforwardly no less than once per day for seven days.

7. Concede your missteps and weaknesses

Fathers and spouses if it's not too much trouble, concede your errors. Nobody is great and it goes such a ton further to concede you committed an error and that you are heartbroken. I realize it isn't in that frame of mind to do this, yet doing this is one of the most outstanding characteristics of good dads and extraordinary spouses.

Noteworthy Stage: When you are off-base. Just own it and apologize. Perceive how much faster everybody continues on from the fight.

8. Ponder the higher perspective

Take a couple of seconds and contemplate the 10,000 foot view and the objectives of a family and what you believe they should bear in mind about growing up.

Noteworthy stage: Whenever there is an issue you need to bring up with the children, contemplate will it matter in seven days, a month, a year, in 5 years? In the event that the response is indeed, discuss it. Assuming the response is no allowed the children to be kids and partake in the time and time of life you are in.

9. Take Family Excursions

Take family excursions. It makes recollections. It assists everybody with getting away from regular stressors. Take get-aways. They don't need to be intricate or cost huge amount of cash. Setting up camp is dependably a minimal expense get-away in the event that you are searching for one! Do some setting up camp artworks for youngsters, play fun setting up camp games,and set free.

Significant stage: Plunk down as a family and discuss your next family excursion. Begin arranging where to go and what to do.

10. Go on dates with your significant other

Spouses take your significant other on dates and plan it! Get the sitter, pick something that she jumps at the chance to do, and proceed to invest energy as a team. So frequently guardians get so enveloped with one another that we neglect to sustain our relationship.

Significant stage: Plan a date with your better half for the following week.
That's basically it! These straightforward things you can do to be a decent dad and spouse. What might you add to the rundown? Share in the remarks!

CHAPTER TWO

Characteristics of a Decent Spouse That Tell He's
Marriage Material

Some could say that when you find the ideal individual,
you'll be aware. It resembles a light going off in your
mind! Yet, some of the time, what your head and heart
need in the ideal accomplice are totally various things.
Having norms is fundamental for meeting your first love.
That is the reason we'll examine the top characteristics
of a decent spouse.
* Do you continue to wind up with men who mightn't?
* Folks who mistreat you?
* Somebody who causes you to really regret yourself?
The secret to keeping away from these harmful
connections is to find the ideal relationship is to quit
settling and begin searching for a man who is spouse
material. You need somebody you can see yourself with
until the end of your life.

However, what makes up great characteristics in a
man? Continue to peruse to figure out the fundamental
characteristics of a decent spouse.
What makes a decent spouse?
At the point when you make a rundown of what compels
a decent spouse, you'll find that you believe he should
have similar characteristics as your closest companion:
* Steady love

* Shared interests
* Regard
* Sympathy
* The capacity to have a great time together

These are incredible starting points for a delightful relationship, yet there are additional characteristics of a decent spouse to search for in the event that you're attempting to track down the man of your fantasies. Would you like to know the best qualities to search for in a spouse? Continue to peruse to figure out the 20 most significant characteristics of a decent spouse who will satisfy you.

Coming up next are recorded a couple of fundamental characteristics of a decent spouse. Realizing these characteristics can assist you with interpreting assuming that you have tracked down the man of your fantasies. Obviously, your man can be much more than the characteristics recorded here. In any case, these are a portion of the usually noticed qualities of a decent man. In this way, read along to understand what makes a decent spouse.

1. Incredible correspondence

Correspondence is the underpinning of any extraordinary relationship.
An accomplice who imparts knows how to communicate their sentiments, wants, and needs without flying off the handle or upset.

Correspondence additionally helps decline your feelings of anxiety, increment your close to home intimacy,deepen your relationship, and cause you to feel appreciated and figured out by your accomplice. Incredible correspondence is one of the most mind-blowing characteristics of a man.

2. He sees you as his accomplice.
At the point when you get hitched, you become far beyond better halves - you are accomplices forever. The characteristics of a decent spouse are clear when you see that he sees you as his accomplice and his equivalent. He believes you should partake in direction, esteems your contribution on his objectives, and offers his existence with you.

3. A craving to accompany you
One sign that your sweetheart is marriage material is assuming he's as of now clarified that he needs you and just you.
Quality men don't mess around with your heart. Your sweetheart will show you he's prepared for genuine love on the off chance that you are the main lady he's engaging sincerely.

4. He is reliable

Trust is one of the top great characteristics in a man. Research shows that a reliable accomplice will cause you to feel more satisfied in your relationship.

Believing your man implies you realize you can impart anything to him without being judged. Trust likewise assists you with expanding weakness and love.
A relationship where you have a solid sense of reassurance, quiet, and ready to be open to your companion will develop further marriage.

5. Discussing what's to come

One of the top characteristics of a man that will show you he's significant other material is assuming he discusses your future together. This will show that he's reasoning long haul and is similarly as invigorated for responsibility as you are.
Assuming that your beau discusses beginning a family, moving in together, and getting hitched, you realize that he as of now has the qualities to search for in a spouse.

6. He makes you giggle.

A man who knows how to make you snicker is what a spouse ought to be.
There are many advantages to having humor in your relationship.
Making each other chuckle can de-raise expected contentions, lower pressure, and adds to sensations of help and fulfillment in connections.
Couples who know how to snicker together are bound to remain cheerful and in affection.

Research found that sharing humor yields a higher likelihood of relationship achievement and permits couples to trade positive feelings together.

7. You share basic beliefs

Opposites are drawn toward each other, however that doesn't mean your relationship is bound to be sound. One of the best characteristics of a decent spouse is shared qualities. Search for somebody who is enthusiastic about exactly the same things you are, particularly with regards to your ethical compass. Research shows that couples who share confidence are bound to see their relationship as extraordinary.

Additionally, couples who exercise together are bound to remain inspired. Research in regards to sorting out alone As opposed to working out with your sweetheart uncovered that just 76% of single members finished the program contrasted with 95% of couples. Likewise, all 95% of couples kept up with their weight reduction contrasted with the 66% of single members.

8. Your companions love him

Have you at any point had a companion let you know the individual got a terrible energy from your crush? Here and there your companions can see your relationship more clear than you can. They aren't head over heels creating oxytocin as are you.

A decent man will act naturally when he's around your companion. He won't put on an act for them.

On the off chance that your companion coexists well with your dearest companions and families and your friends and family are offering both of you go-ahead, chances are you have viewed as the one.

9.He shows appreciation

Appreciation and appreciation may not seem like fundamental characteristics of a decent spouse, yet going a long time without somebody recognizing your adoration and support can deplete. You might feel like you're carrying on with an unpleasant life.

As a spouse, you get after your home and husband while possibly focusing on kids or working a regular work. This can debilitate.

These are astounding motivations to search for spouse characteristics rotating around articulations of appreciation and appreciation.

CHAPTER THREE

Top Features of a Decent Dad and Husband

Being an astounding father is more than accommodating the family. See the characteristics of a decent dad and spouse and see what character qualities make the biggest difference.

Great fathers are surrounding us, wouldn't you say?

Astounding fathers who awaken around mid night to change diapers, to make sure we can have a couple of additional minutes to continue to rest. Fathers who end a long work day still anxious to play pursue, regardless of whether it implies a tad.
I'm thankful my children have an extraordinary father, and I know I'm in good company.

 A large number of us have no clue about how we'd get past life as a parent without the accomplices we have in our lives. I recall when my better half gone for work and I was distant from everyone else with the children — this caused me to acknowledge the amount I depended on him.

The thing is, in the midst of all the franticness of having children, it's barely noticeable that we are so lucky to have these folks close by. As a matter of fact, connections are in many cases the first to be disregarded, or turns into the wellspring of disappointment.

That is the reason I needed to list these numerous characteristics, so we can recall how great we have it. No father is great — similarly as no mother is — except for I'm willing to wager that your person has numerous while perhaps not this large number of characteristics:

1. Exceeds all expectations for his loved ones

Have you seen that business of the dad moving before his home, rehearsing team promoter moves with his daughter? Or on the other hand the representation of a father dozing on the edge of the bed since his youngster had taken more than 90% of it?

Fathers as of now battle with a weighty disgrace in parenthood, one that says they lose a piece of their masculinity when they to such an extent as support their children.

However here are fathers ready to spruce up like Elsa so their little girls could be Anna, or the individuals who stay up practically the entire night to figure out how to calm the child so we can rest.

One of the most outstanding characteristics of a decent dad and spouse is exceeding everyone's expectations for his family, not on the grounds that he needs to, but since he needs to.

We'll handle one noteworthy propensity each day that you can carry out immediately to definitely change the manner in which you bring up your kid. This is your opportunity to challenge yourself and roll out the improvements you've been importance to make.

2. Kind

Great fathers are kind of their accomplices and children. Being a decent father doesn't mean placing his necessities last constantly or forfeiting his own bliss and interests. Indeed, he thinks about his requirements and needs ("I need to watch soccer on the television"), yet knows about what might satisfy you and the children too.
He's the father who urges you to take up a past side interest and will plan it in his own schedule so he can accompany the children. He envisions what it resembles to be from your point of view so he can more readily comprehend what you're going through.
Kind dads acknowledge what their families feel and give their best for help them in a good manner.

3. Steps up

A blissful home method the two guardians step up, whether running the family or really focusing on the children. One of the most outstanding characteristics of a decent dad and spouse is the tendency to step up to the plate — to "take care of business" since it necessities to finish.
Since nobody likes to pester an individual parent about investing energy with the children, or doing his part at

home. These exercises are natural to a decent father who chooses to take them on himself, without a second thought or resentment.

4. Attempts… and continues on

Great fathers don't surrender, particularly with regards to fostering areas of strength for a with their children. It's excessively simple to have a go at something — for example, to mitigate a child or discipline a baby just to withdraw when it didn't work.
In any case, a decent father sticks with it. He keeps mitigating the child, in any event, while giving her over to you would get the job done in a moment. All things considered, by what other means will he realize what the child likes assuming he surrenders the initial time? By what other means will the child feel good in his arms when she's scarcely with him?
Great fathers realize that this is essential for the job he pursued. He doesn't hand every one of the obligations to another person, yet readily takes on as much as you.

5. Involved

We some of the time whine that fathers aren't as engaged with the children as we are. Simultaneously, it's likewise significant for us not to regard fathers as the "partner," somebody we delegate errands to while we run others.
Since fathers aren't sitters — they're co-guardians who ought to be as involved.

Involved fathers know as much about their children as we do. They realize which toy the child loves best on a buggy ride and what projects the children are doing at school. They plan days off to go to games and science fairs and alternate carrying the children to the specialist.

6. Thankful

We as a whole need to feel recognized and appreciated, particularly in the main part of the difficulties of being a parent.
Astounding fathers are more than appreciative for all we do and for the job we play in our associations and everyday life. Little signals like an embrace and a "thank you," to greater ones like taking you to the films, are a portion of the manners in which fathers show appreciation for their accomplices.
Appreciation additionally stretches out into realizing how genuinely honored and plentiful their lives are. They're appreciative for individuals in their lives and rush to see what is going on.

7. Adoring

Ask any mother what separates her life partner from the pack, and many will highlight the adoration and warmth he has for his loved ones.
Of the characteristics of a decent dad and spouse, love by a long shot transcends them all. Astonishing fathers love us with all that they have, and it pours out in all they say and accomplish for us.

They appreciate playing with the children and will track down innovative ways of having a great time. However, they'll likewise endure the fits of rage, in any event, when they test their understanding, knowing that that is what their children need from them right now.

Great fathers don't offer empty talk and "know" they love their family — they show it in significant ways, consistently.

Characteristics and Ways of being a Decent Spouse and Father

What are the characteristics of a decent spouse? Does your ideal life accomplice have to have a steady employment, an unlimited financial balance, or an undying adoration?

Whether you're a solitary woman who is searching for the right spouse, a wedded lady... this article is for you.

CHAPTER FOUR

Ways of being a Responsible Spouse and Father

What are the ways to be a responsible spouse and father? Does your ideal life accomplice have to have a steady employment, an unlimited financial balance, or an undying adoration?
Whether you're a solitary woman who is searching for the right spouse, a wedded lady… this article is for you.

Let this rundown of ways guide your marriage, family, and life in general.

1. Warmth

He gives you enough warmth as his significant other. He prefers you, he's enamored with you, he kisses and embraces you - he's sweet and heartfelt to you regardless of how long have passed.

2. Freedom

He doesn't depend on his folks or your folks to furnish you and your kids with food, cover, and different necessities as a family.

3. Authority

He is solid, has drive, and knows how to guide and lead your family to the correct way. For this reason you will submit yourself to him as his significant other. He is likewise a decent good example for your kids.

4. Dependability

He doesn't swindle. He doesn't play with different ladies. He is frightened of losing you.

5. Self esteem

He adores himself as he cherishes you and your loved ones. He endeavors to be content and solid so he can continuously show up for yourself as well as your kids.

6. Trust

He believes in you. He doesn't deal with you like somebody who is a miscreant and can't be relied upon. He additionally depends you with all his property, cash, and repeating pay.

7. Information

Regarding #6, he really confides in you since he understands you better than any other person. He applied endeavors to know you. He knows your number one tone, music, food, place - and he likewise knows your demeanor and every little thing about you.

8. Honesty

He tells the truth and straightforward. He believes you and you can likewise trust him consequently.

9. Appreciation

He doesn't neglect to much obliged. He values even the seemingly insignificant details you accomplish for him. Furthermore, hence, you are more motivated to serve and cherish him since you realize that your endeavors won't be squandered.

10. Persistence

He doesn't blow up with you, your children, and others. He doesn't blow up when there are issues or inconveniences. He can endure torment or persevere through enduring on the grounds that he knows that every one of them are simply preliminaries that ought to make him more grounded instead of more fragile.

11. Ingenuity

He is industrious and reliable. He never stops until he accomplishes his fantasy for yourself as well as your loved ones. He isn't deterred and he doesn't surrender even in the event that his few endeavors fizzle. He will proceed with regardless of what amount of time hard or how it will require to give your family a more promising time to come.

12. Discretion

He has self-restraint. He knows how to control himself to stay away from avarices, tipsiness, inactivity, desire, and different indecencies that will place your lives in wretchedness.

13. Insight

He can recognize common decency from wrong. He's not a uninformed blockhead who keeps on perpetrating bad behaviors, like lying, cheating, being unreliable, being sluggish and it are simply alright to feel that those.

14. Understanding

He grasps you. He grasps himself. He comprehends what he says. He grasps his decisions or choices. He has understanding since he practices and encounters what he teaches.

15. Empathy

He comprehends you since he is caring. He feels your satisfaction, subsequently, he maintains that you should remain cheerful. He additionally feels your bitterness and enduring, in this way, he believes should do all that to facilitate your aggravation.

16. Pardoning

He isn't wrathful. He doesn't record and think back on your previous oversights. He knows how to excuse, neglect, and forward to carry on with a cheerful existence with you and your kids.

17. Exemplary nature

He dismisses evil. He withdraws from sins, malignance, and defilement. He makes the wisest decision, and to that end he is honored. His honorable activities carry great karma to you and your kids' lives.

18. Equity

He is fair and just. He won't ever cause you to feel that existence with him is so uncalled for.

19. Regard

He regards you as a lady. However they might be not the same as his, he regards your own perspectives and choices. He additionally knows how to regard himself.

20. Satisfaction

He is blissful and satisfied with you. For his purposes, you are his blessing from heaven. He never wishes to have different spouses or paramours. He never begrudges different men, on the grounds that, as far as he might be concerned, he feels like he is the most fortunate man on Earth since he has you.

21. Magnanimity

He has a feeling of penance. He contemplates you and your kids first before himself. He surrenders his own things for you. He spends his cash, significant investment for the entire family, not just for himself. You won't track down any motivation to call him a narrow minded individual.

22. Righteousness

He is a Divine being dreading individual. He complies with God's precepts and practices His lessons throughout everyday life. He carries you and your children nearer to God.

23. Cheerfulness

He generally sees a decent future with you regardless of how troublesome the present is. He doesn't handily lose trust in you regardless of your shortcomings and deficiencies. He generally gives you great and inspirational tones that assist your home and family with becoming more joyful, more certain, and consistently continue to go regardless of how troublesome life is.

24. Loyalty

He is devoted to you. He trusts in you. He doesn't have to see you all an opportunity to trust you. He doesn't have to have a deep understanding of you to be sure with you. His confidence is in real life - his dedication causes him to pay attention to you, love you, and penance for you.

25. Constancy

He really buckles down for you. He is spurred to attempt to construct a more promising time to come for your youngsters. He doesn't sit around idly yet persistently and enthusiastically take care of his business or work with the goal that your family will constantly have something to procure from now on.

26. Thoughtfulness

He is a compassionate man. He generally needs to assist you and see you with grinning. He isn't discourteous. He would rather not cause you any physical, mental and close to home mischief.

27. Delicacy

He is delicate with your psyche, heart, and body. At the point when you commit botches, he reproaches you delicately and tranquilly, not irately.

28. Tranquility

He could do without squabbles and trivial battles. He doesn't contend with you when you are not in a decent mode. He gives you existence at whatever point you want them. He carves out the ideal time to talk and pay attention to you to determine issues so both of you can have a decent night's rest.

29. Modesty

He isn't pleased and self-important. He is a resilient individual intellectually, genuinely and profoundly - and for that reason he can stand to go low to beat pride and support consideration, harmony, and satisfaction to individuals around him.

30. Acknowledgment

He acknowledges you for what your identity is. He doesn't pass judgment on you. He doesn't drive you to turn into an individual that you're not. Be that as it may, he keeps on moving you to develop as a superior individual. He moves you to improve by doing and showing you the change he maintains that you should be.

31. Support

He upholds you in your undertakings to be a superior and more effective lady. He additionally upholds your kids in their own decisions in life as long as he sees them be noble and make them genuinely blissful.

32. Genuine affection

At last, he is genuinely infatuated with you. He knows it, he makes certain about it, he feels it, and he generally educates you regarding his actual sentiments even in irregular environments.

The characteristics of a decent spouse which I've recently referenced above might be difficult to come by among men. Nonetheless, on the off chance that a man is genuinely infatuated with a lady or his wife,he will endeavor to foster those characteristics above. Moreover, isn't genuine affection ties every one of them in wonderful solidarity, right?

CHAPTER FIVE

Step by step instructions to be a Moderate Spouse

Marriage isn't simply a legitimate understanding yet a deep rooted responsibility. At the point when you wed somebody, you guarantee with everything that is in you and brain that you will accompany your mate and esteem your adoration for better or for more awful, for more extravagant or less fortunate, in ailment and wellbeing, as long as you live.
Actually marital promises are difficult to keep. You can continuously wear your wedding band to show your faithfulness to your life partner, however keeping such dedication in your heart, brain, and deeds is another story. Marriage isn't about images and services yet it's about activities and practices.

Assuming that you love your significant other, you need to show her that you are attempting to be a decent and, surprisingly, a superior spouse consistently. Indeed, it's far from simple or easy. Yet, assuming you know what to do, you can as of now begin defining your course to that objective at this point. In the event that you have no clue about how to be a superior companion, the following are methods for being a decent spouse to direct you.

1. Love your significant other as you love yourself.

At the point when you get hitched, you and your significant other become one tissue. Thus, you ought to cherish your better half as you love yourself - you ought to deal with your significant other as yourself. Never hurt your significant other; never hurt yourself. Recall that you can't adore your significant other in the event that you can't cherish yourself. What's more, you can't adore yourself on the off chance that you couldn't in fact cherish your significant other.

At the end of the day, assuming that you love your better half, love your body. Try not to be a boozer or an epicurean. Try not to place yourself in affliction and serious peril. At the point when you're solid, your significant other will definitely be blissful as she won't be stressed over you.

2. Partake in the food she prepares.

However long it isn't noxious or unsafe to your wellbeing, then appreciate and value the food she prepares or heats. You can speak the truth about the taste - it will assist her with getting to the next level. Be that as it may, regardless of how it tastes, don't quit valuing her.

3. Excel at keeping oneself quiet.

Love shows restraint. Subsequently, to be a decent spouse, develop your understanding consistently. Figure out how to control your indignation and keep yourself quiet regardless of anything else. In the midst of battling and contentions, be developed and be the carrier of serenity and harmony.

4. Be an extraordinary pioneer by being an incredible worker.

Men should lead their own spouses. In any case, how might you make your significant other trust and follow you in the event that you are not dependable and solid? Hence, show your significant other that you can be relied upon. Show her that you are a dependable pioneer.
A dependable pioneer is somebody who leads by activities, not by simple discussions. He isn't bossy. He doesn't lead by just giving directions however a worker chief who shows others how its done.

5. Be a superior child in-regulation and kin in-regulation.

To have a more joyful and more grounded marriage, give your all to satisfy your in-laws and kin. Recollect that you have previously turned into a piece of their family, and as a their relative, you need to make an agreeable relationship with them.

In the event that you love your better half yet disdain her family, and assuming you are thoughtful and liberal to your significant other yet you are discourteous to her family, then what sort of a man would you say you are?

6. Bite the bullet

Pride ruins connections. It causes frivolous battles and burns through quality time in your marriage. If you have any desire to be a superior life partner, be a more modest individual. Whether it's your issue or hers, forever be quick to offer harmony and request pardoning. Be sensible so you can raise your significant other and your marriage.

7. Recollect the significant dates.

Remember your wedding commemoration, her birthday, and different days which are extraordinary to her. Also, beside recalling that them, give something that will astonish your significant other and satisfy her on that exceptionally extraordinary day.

8. Be faithful.

Never at any point cheat. It's untrustworthy as well as unlawful in specific nations. Keep your marriage promise, not just on the grounds that you could do without to be detained or be fined, however certainly in light of the fact that you basically love your significant other and you believe she should have an accomplice who cherishes her and just her.

9. Keep your eyes just on her.

It could be challenging to do yet the eye is the light of the body (read Matthew 6:22-24) and it is likewise viewed as the window to your spirit. Subsequently, if you need to be the best spouse to your significant other, don't allow your eyes to sin. It very well might be your eyes that are just erring, however over the long run, it might reach and ruin your spirit. Consequently, the most effective way to keep yourself from cheating is to forestall it before it arrives at your eyes.

10. Keep on charming her.

Keep the sentiment and pleasantness alive regardless of how long you've been hitched to her. Date her, compose love notes for her, and deal with her like a sovereign or a princess. Rather than overthinking assuming that she actually adores you, center around making her experience passionate feelings for you again and again.

11. Regard her.

Continuously regard your significant other. Recall that she's your significant other. Consequently, you ought to regard everything about her, her perspectives, her privileges, your relationship with her, her parenthood to your kids, and, surprisingly, her significant other - yourself. Try not to quit regarding her, regardless of whether you figure she doesn't merit it.

12. Simply trust her.

Young ladies believe that their folks should trust them. They could do without you to consider negative things about them. They don't believe men should regard them as a messy and conniving individual. Thus, on the off chance that you have no verification that your significant other can't be relied upon, then trust her and quit getting unreliable or jumpy.

13. Center around making yourself reliable.

Rather than questioning your significant other to an extreme and allowing yourself to get distrustful, focus on building your better half's confidence in you. Center around doing right by her that you can be relied upon. Fabricate trust in your marriage by beginning to assemble it from yourself.

14. Keep no record of wrongs.

Did your better half commit errors before? Try not to raise those issues again to shield yourself when you battle. Continue on from the past, particularly on the off chance that you two have previously settled them and you have proactively excused her. Raising previous issues just makes vast contentions.

15. Praise your adoration with reality.

Marriage is more joyful and better when couples don't have anything to stow away from one another.

Consequently, let reality wins in your relationship. Be straightforward and legitimate consistently. Disclose your large mysteries so you can liberate yourself and keep on adoring without clutching lies.

16. Give existence.

There are ladies who could do without to talk when they are frantic at you. If you're the sort of a man who has any desire to determine issues in your relationship right away however your accomplice isn't, then, at that point, don't compel her to talk. Figure out how to give her an existence to chill off and ponder the issues. Be patient and understanding.

17. Figure out how to set aside cash.

Quit drinking an excessive amount of liquor and eating a lot of meat. Quit smoking, betting and different indecencies. Quit purchasing unessential things. Set aside cash and work harder to develop your pay and abundance. This will clearly fulfill your better half and kids.

18. Construct your own home.

You genuinely must have your own home. You don't have to construct a manor, however a good house, whether possessed or rented, that will give you and your better half freedom from your folks will surely assist your marriage and family with developing.

19. Be a decent dad.

Moms have unadulterated love for their youngsters. If you have any desire to be a decent spouse, be a decent dad. Being a decent parent isn't just about giving all that your youngsters need or need. To be a decent father, you need to show your kids a feeling of discipline. To move them, be a good example by having self-restraint.

20. Be magnanimous.

Have a feeling of penance. Show your better half and kids that you can forfeit things for them. Reschedule that conference to go to your girl's school show. Drop that b-ball game with your pack to give way to a heartfelt supper date with your significant other. Remain solid and don't become ill, so you will continuously be accessible to your loved ones.

21. Be appreciative.

Be appreciative for the love and care your significant other is giving you. Tell her how lovely she is. Advise her how fortunate and favored you are to have her in your life. Eliminate any jealousy in your heart. Try not to look at your better half or your wedded life to others out there. Be cheerful and content.

22. Be caring and delicate.

You shouldn't just be delicate with your significant other truly yet additionally genuinely and intellectually. Most couples have inverse mentalities and lifestyles. In the event that you believe your significant other should change into a superior individual, don't power and rush her - it's so upsetting. Simply be delicate and let her vibe a sort and warm climate. You will be astonished the way that it will help her change for the better.Speaking of thoughtfulness and delicacy, don't drive your significant other to engage in sexual relations with you. Despite the fact that she has a conjugal commitment with you, it's actually better on the off chance that you can guarantee that both of you appreciate it. On the off chance that she's dependably not in that frame of mind, then you must be imaginative and effectively get her in that frame of mind.

23. Be a superior audience.

Try not to go on and on. Be a decent spouse by listening all the more frequently to your significant other. Be a superior spouse by accomplishing something in view of what you have paid attention to. On the off chance that you hear issues from your better half, assist her with settling them. Assuming you hear her asking something from you, give it to her. Recollect that a superior audience is definitely not a simple audience, however a practitioner.

24. Know her.

What's her number one tone, food, blossom, spot, film, or tune? What makes her so cheerful or miserable? What are her objectives and dreams throughout everyday life? What does she believe you should turn into? You ought to realize those things to cherish her and satisfy her. Observe that knowing is cherishing.

25. Grasp her.

Whether it's aggravation or happiness, feel what she feels. Allow her to understand that you likewise feel miserable when she's miserable - and cheerful when she's blissful. Allow her to understand that your hearts are associated and won't ever be separated. Try not to kill her straightforward delights throughout everyday life. Assuming she appreciates singing, join her despite the fact that it's abnormal and she's unnatural.

26. Safeguard her.

Be her legend. Safeguard her from actual risk as well as from mental, close to home, and, surprisingly, otherworldly risks. At the end of the day, don't give her psychological pressure, don't make her extremely upset, and don't bring her into enticements. Carry her nearer to God.

27. Support her.

She loves to cook and dreams to possess her own eatery? Assist her with satisfying her fantasy. Does she cherish being a homemaker yet get excessively fed up with dealing with your home and youngsters? Give your significant other a decent back rub to help her unwind and revive around evening time.

28. Be confident.

Trust is the point at which you keep on being sure representing things to come regardless of your current battles. To be a superior spouse, don't simply trust, yet be confident. All in all, be confident regardless of how troublesome your current battles are. Try not to tell your significant other she's sad when she battles to improve. Try not to say that your marriage is sad when both of you are still attached attempting to save your relationship. Recall that as long as you live there is trust.

29. Be devoted.

Confidence proves our expectation. To be an incredible mate, you shouldn't just expectation yet additionally effectively reinforce your expectation. Trusting that your significant other will change into a superior individual without supporting and rousing her is having trust without confidence. Trusting that your relationship will endure ceaselessly yourself from lying and cheating doesn't make you reliable by the same token. Effectively approve your expectation - this is what's truly going on with devotion!

30. Show her what genuine affection truly is.

At long last, to be an incredible husband to your companion, let her experience what genuine romance is. You can show your genuine romance by putting forth a valiant effort to follow the tips above. Being an extraordinary or even a decent husband truly is troublesome. However, in the event that you really love your significant other, you can forfeit extraordinary things to change yourself to be a superior individual so you can be a superior spouse to your better half and a superior dad to your kids.

At the point when you love really, you produce life's most noteworthy ethics, like persistence, thoughtfulness, empathy, delicacy, lowliness, and restraint. Thusly, regardless of the fact that it is so challenging to be a superior life partner, as long as you have genuine romance in your heart for your significant other, improving as a spouse will just work out easily.

CHAPTER SIX

An Amazing Spouse is an Amazing Dad: Ways Of being an Amazing Father

If you have any desire to be an amazing spouse, be an amazing dad!
Some think that it is just the obligation of moms to bring up the kids, while the dads' obligation is just to accommodate their necessities. In any case, this isn't accurate. Fathers need to have dynamic support in the existences of their children as well. This will decidedly affect them as they grow up.
All in all, how might you be an amazing father? In the event that you are another dad and you are as yet grabbing in obscurity, here are a successful ways of getting it done.

1. Be an amazing supplier.

Most families these days have the two guardians turning out as of now for better monetary security. Whether or not your children's mom is working or not, ensure that you are doing your part competently. Regardless of whether your compensation isn't all that huge, for however long you are bending over backward to address their issues, most likely your children will see the value in it.

2. Invest energy with your kids routinely.

Make more often than not that your kids are as yet youthful. Opportunity will come when they will have lives of their own and you'd miss them around. That is the reason, regardless of how occupied you are working, make time to bond with them. I value one father I had chatted with before who let me know he goes through thirty minutes with every one of his children consistently.

3. Be accessible to them.

Whenever your children welcome you to watch their class presentation, go to their graduation, or any occasion they think about unique, don't miss it. At the point when they are debilitated or just requiring somebody to converse with, be accessible. Your presence is vital to encourage your kids.

4. Set a genuine model.

In the event that you don't believe your kids should gain indecencies, such as smoking and alcohol drinking, then don't have them as well. On the off chance that you believe they should be polite, diligent, and restrained, be their good example. The most ideal way to show your children something is by showing it to them.

5. Be uncompromising with house rules.

In the event that you set house rules, for example, a time limitation, TV watching timetables, and house tasks, be firm and reliable with them. Try not to yield to impulses and reasons (except if substantial). Make relating ramifications for disappointments to keep these guidelines. For example, the individuals who return home past the check in time would be grounded all weekend long.

6. Show restraint toward them.

It is typical for kids to bother now and again. By and by, regardless of the amount they are driving you insane, don't become annoyed with them. Never hit them bitterly in light of the fact that that would be actual maltreatment. Indeed, I think hitting might be utilized for discipline, yet it ought not be too hard, should be done sensibly, and ought to be clarified for the children why they needed to get it.

7. Try not to be excessively extreme.

Discipline should be ingrained in the family, yet I don't believe being too severe on your children would help. They might submit to you currently out of dread, however when they have the opportunity to be free, they would disrupt free from the norms you had set. A ton of companions I realized who had come from severe families wound up extremely freed.

8. Right their errors.

As a parent, it is your obligation to ensure your kids will grow up as upstanding and productive members of society. In this manner, as soon as now, don't be careless in rectifying them when they get rowdy. For example, assuming you hear them reviling, you should quickly address it by making sense of why it is terrible and cautioning them of getting rebuffed on the off chance that you hear it once more.

9. Figure out how to pay attention to them.

Indeed, guardians might know better, however to keep away from your children from getting far off from you, figure out how to pay attention to their reasons. You might be the top of the family, yet your kids have their own contemplations. Prior to establishing or chastening them for something they have done, let them account for themselves first. Then, at that point, on the off chance that their explanation isn't legitimate, you might continue with the result.

10. Be strong of their fantasies.

Rather than pushing your kids to seek after a profession of your decision, let them follow their enthusiasm. Urge them to take up a higher education or a task apparently seeking to win over their affections. Along these lines, they will have a superior possibility prevailing in their picked fields since they are content with what they do.

11. Permit them to choose for themselves.

However youthful as they seem to be, train your children to be autonomous and unequivocal. They ought to figure out how to settle on what they need, for example, the dinner to arrange or the shade of shoes to purchase. At the point when they grow up, they won't be quickly bossed around by individuals encompassing them.

12. Show that you are pleased with them.

Your appreciation as a father is no joking matter for your youngsters. Tell them the amount you are glad for them. Value them before others and never come close them to different youngsters. These will assist with helping their confidence.

13. Love their mother.

One of the ways of being a decent dad is by cherishing and regarding the mother of your children. With the developing number of broken families in the public eye, your kids might have tension that your family might fall to pieces as well.Safeguard them from this trepidation by showing them that your marriage is based on major areas of strength for an of adoration.

14. Stand as the profound head of the family.

As the top of the family, one of your essential obligations is driving your youngsters to follow the Master. Set an illustration of how a faithful way of life ought to be lived. Lead them through family dedications and petitioning God time. Regularly practice it of going to the congregation as a family too.

Man Up

It isn't not difficult to be a dad, and at times, the obligations that accompany this job become hard to bear. In any case, for the love of your family, reinforce your will, plan for the future, and with the assistance of God and your significant other, endeavor to be the best father that you can be.

CHAPTER SEVEN

Qualities of a Decent Spouse in the Holy book

1. Independence
2. Affection
3. Dedication and commitment
4. Leadership
5. Self-love
6. Trust and confidence
7. Appreciation
8. Godliness
9. Spirituality
10. Honesty
11. Forgiveness
12. Righteousness
13. Contentment
14. Courage
15. Patience
16. Great influence
17. Self-control
18. Fidelity
19. Wisdom
20. Altruism
21. Genuine romance

CONCLUSION

What makes a decent spouse?
What characteristics make a decent spouse, and do the qualities of an ideal man exist?

The qualities of a decent spouse incorporate reliability, correspondence, regard, and obviously - love!
Your companion doesn't must have each of the great characteristics in a man recorded above to be a superb, cherishing accomplice to you. Development is a significant piece of affection.
Inasmuch as your companion is focused on development and correspondence, you will have a great marriage in front of you.

As may be obvious, there are numerous characteristics we can be appreciative for. It's not entirely obvious that we are so lucky to have these folks, particularly when life feels furious and we're consumed with the everyday assignments.However, great fathers are surrounding us. They're the ones who do an amazing job for their families and are kind of how others feel or what they could require. They step up to the plate, and don't surrender regardless of whether something sort out on the primary attempt.

Great fathers are engaged with day to day life and consistently show their appreciation. What's more,

generally significant, they love us with all that they have
— even in the littlest of signals like changing a diaper
around mid night.